HOW DO
CHAMELEONS
CHANGE COLOR?

ALONSO GARCIA

New York

Published in 2018 by The Rosen Publishing Group, Inc.
29 East 21st Street, New York, NY 10010

Copyright © 2018 by The Rosen Publishing Group, Inc.

First Edition

Editor: Theresa Morlock
Book Design: Tanya Dellaccio

Photo Credits: Cover, pp. 1, 3, 4–6, 8–10, 12–16, 18–20, 22–24 Harkamal Nijjar/Getty Images; p. 5 (top) belizar/Shutterstock.com; p. 5 (bottom) Vladimirkarp/Shutterstock.com; p. 6 Angela N Perryman/Shutterstock.com; p. 7 Stefan Huwiler/imageBROKER/Getty Images; p. 8 URTIMUD PRODUCTION/Shutterstock.com; p. 9 (both) Nick Henn/Shutterstock.com; p. 11 Auscape/Universal Images Group/Getty Images; p. 12 Baishev/Shutterstock.com; p. 13 (top) GUDKOV ANDREY/Shutterstock.com; pp. 13 (bottom), 17 Cathy Keifer/Shutterstock.com; p. 15 (top) Josh Zed/Shutterstock.com; p. 15 (bottom) Ian Schofield/Shutterstock.com; p. 16 Fedor Selivanov/Shutterstock.com; p. 19 (top) Anna_G/Shutterstock.com; p. 19 (bottom) Jan Bures/Shutterstock.com; p. 20 Stephen Clarke/Shutterstock.com; p. 21 Danita Delimont/Gallo Images/Getty Images; p. 22 Geoffrey Newland/Shutterstock.com

Cataloging-in-Publication Data
Names: Garcia, Alonso.
Title: How do chameleons change color? / Alonso Garcia.
Description: New York : PowerKids Press, 2018. | Series: How life science works | Includes index.
Identifiers: ISBN 9781508156734 (pbk.) | ISBN 9781508156437 (library bound) | ISBN 9781508156314 (6 pack)
Subjects: LCSH: Chameleons–Juvenile literature. | Camouflage (Biology)–Juvenile literature. | Adaptation (Biology)–Juvenile literature.
Classification: LCC QL666.L23 G37 2018 | DDC 597.95'6–dc23

Manufactured in the United States of America

CPSIA Compliance Information: Batch #BS17PK For Further Information contact Rosen Publishing, New York, New York at 1-800-237-9932

CONTENTS

BEAUTIFUL AND BIZARRE

What's cooler than a chameleon? There are few animals as eye-catching as this startlingly colorful reptile. Their long, sticky tongue, bulging eyes, and amazing patterns set them apart as some of the weirdest-looking lizards in the world. But the most **extraordinary** thing about chameleons is their ability to change color.

How exactly do chameleons change the color of their skin? Why do they do it? Is it a form of **camouflage** or a way to attract a **mate**? Can a chameleon's color tell you what mood it's in? Let's find out!

Some people keep chameleons as pets and can watch the animals change color right before their eyes!

CHAMELEON BASICS

There are more than 150 different species, or kinds, of chameleons. Most of them live in the deserts or rainforests of Africa or Madagascar. Some chameleons, such as the *Brookesia micra*, are tiny, measuring only 1 inch (2.5 cm) long! Others, like the Parson's chameleon, can be as big as a cat.

Chameleons are arboreal, which means they live in trees. Most chameleons have a prehensile tail, or a tail that can grab onto things. They also have five digits on each foot. Their special feet help them grasp branches.

CHAMELEONS USE THEIR STRONG TAILS TO GRIP BRANCHES AS THEY CLIMB.

A chameleon's toes are grouped into two parts. They help a chameleon grip things much like a person's thumb and fingers do.

BABY CHAMELEONS

Most female chameleons lay eggs, but some give birth to live young. Those that lay eggs are pregnant for about a month. When it's time to lay their eggs, they climb down from the trees and dig a hole in the ground. They lay their eggs in the hole and then bury them.

Like many other reptiles, chameleons don't raise their young. After the eggs are buried, the young grow inside them for 4 to 24 months. The young must learn to survive on their own after they hatch.

WITHIN DAYS OF HATCHING, YOUNG CHAMELEONS ARE ABLE TO HUNT ON THEIR OWN.

Some chameleons lay clutches, or groups, of up to 100 eggs.

A SPECIAL BODY

A chameleon's body is flat on the sides. Some male members of certain species have horns, which may be used to fight. Chameleons don't have outer ears. Although they can hear, this sense is very weak.

They do, however, have very powerful eyesight. A chameleon can look in two different directions at once! It has cone-shaped eyelids and its eyes can point up, down, backward, or forward. It can look all the way around its body. Chameleons use their super vision to help them snatch their prey with deadly **accuracy**.

CHAMELEONS ARE THE ONLY LIZARDS THAT CAN LOOK IN TWO DIFFERENT DIRECTIONS AT THE SAME TIME.

Chameleons usually eat insects. A few kinds also eat plant parts and even small birds. They capture their prey by snatching it with their strong tongue. Chameleons have a ballistic tongue. This means they're able to shoot it out at high speeds.

A chameleon's tongue can be twice the length of its whole body. The tongue can lash out at speeds up to 13 miles (21 km) per hour. The tip of this tongue is sticky. It fastens to the prey's body so the chameleon can pull it into its mouth.

The rate at which a chameleon shoots out its tongue is the **EQUIVALENT** of a car going from 0 to 60 miles (96.6 km) per hour in a hundredth of a second.

COLOR IS ONLY SKIN DEEP

Chameleons have four layers of skin. The outer layer is transparent, or clear. Inside the layers of skin, there are tiny crystals called nanocrystals, which **reflect** light. The lower skin layers are made up of cells called chromatophores, which **contain** pigment. Pigments are **materials** that absorb, or take in, certain colors of light and reflect others.

Each skin layer holds different pigments. When you see a color, you are seeing light that's reflected by a pigment. For example, chlorophyll, the pigment that makes plants green, absorbs red and blue light and reflects green.

Not all chameleon species have the same color-changing abilities.

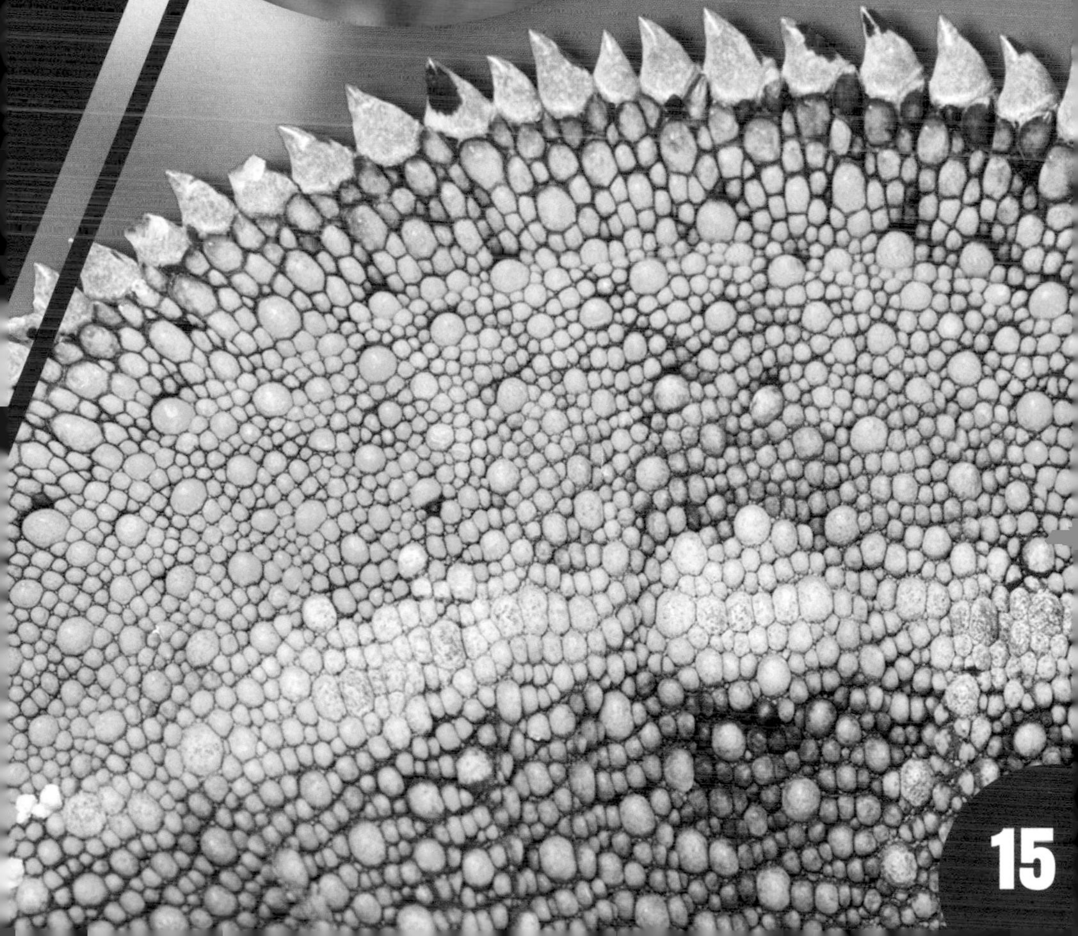

Below the transparent skin layer, the cells of the next skin layer contain red or yellow pigments. The layer below that contains melanin. Melanin is a brown pigment that can reflect blue. The layer of skin below that reflects white.

When a chameleon changes color, its skin cells **shrink** or **expand**. The nanocrystals in the skin move closer together or farther apart, reflecting light and showing color. The colors combine to create the beautiful patterns we see on a chameleon's skin.

It can take less than 20 seconds for a chameleon to change color.

WHY CHANGE COLORS?

People once thought that chameleons changed colors to match whatever they were nearest to. We now know this isn't true. Chameleons aren't able to change to just any color. Each species of chameleon has its own patterns and colors.

Sometimes changing color helps a chameleon hide within its surroundings. More often, however, it's used to draw attention to the chameleon or to help it communicate. Color changes are also affected by temperature and sunlight, as well as the animal's mood and level of **stress**.

A CHAMELEON MAY TURN A DARKER COLOR TO ABSORB MORE SUNLIGHT AND WARM UP. IT MAY TURN A LIGHTER COLOR TO COOL DOWN.

COLORFUL COMMUNICATION

One of the main reasons chameleons change color is to communicate with each other. Brightly colored males show off their colors to attract females. A female's colors can show if she accepts a male. Sometimes they can show if she's pregnant. Bright colors are used to warn away enemies and show that a chameleon is powerful.

Chameleons' colors can show their moods. Stress, fear, anger, and excitement can cause a chameleon's colors to shift by sending signals from the animal's brain to its cells.

FEMALE CHAMELEONS CAN CHANGE COLOR BUT DON'T HAVE THE SAME VIBRANT, OR BRIGHT, COLORS THAT MALES DO.

RADIANT REPTILES

The chameleon's ability to change color is one of the most interesting curiosities of the natural world. Just imagine if you could change the color of your skin whenever you were excited, scared, or upset!

For many years, people misunderstood how and why chameleons changed color. Continuing to study these animals can help us understand more about chameleons, but also about how color, light, and cells work. These stunning animals show that, in many ways, we are just beginning to discover the mysteries and marvels of life science.

GLOSSARY

accuracy: The quality of being free of mistakes.

camouflage: Colors or shapes on animals that allow them to blend in with their surroundings.

contain: To hold something.

equivalent: Equal in value, amount, or function.

expand: To become bigger.

extraordinary: Unusual or remarkable.

mate: A partner for making babies, or to come together to make babies.

material: Something from which something else can be made.

reflect: To throw back light, heat, or sound.

shrink: To become smaller.

stress: Something that causes strong feelings of worry.

INDEX

WEBSITES

Due to the changing nature of Internet links, PowerKids Press has developed an online list of websites related to the subject of this book. This site is updated regularly. Please use this link to access the list:
www.powerkidslinks.com/ls/cham